Contents

I am a recycling officer

My name is Bev.
I am a recycling officer.

I work for the South Shropshire District Council. My job is to inform people how to dispose of their rubbish correctly and get them to **recycle** when possible.

I arrive at work at 9 o'clock.

I like to cycle to work. It is better
for the **environment** not to use a car.

On my way in I meet John. He is
a planning inspector and is driving
off to inspect a building site.

Morning meeting

This morning I have a meeting with Victoria and Colin. We are looking at some new posters showing our new recycling scheme and opening times.

We choose which posters we like best. I write down which ones we would like to order.

Planning my day

I have a busy day ahead so I need to plan what I will do. First I make some phone calls. Then the phone rings. The caller wants to know how to **dispose** of an old computer. I tell him to take it to a company who can recycle the old parts in new machines.

We have had a report of some **fly-tipping** in a country lane. Someone has **illegally** dumped lots of rubbish.

I look at a map of the local area to see where it is. I will ring the refuse collectors and ask them to collect it. We will also try to find out who left the rubbish there.

The recycling centre

Next I visit the local recycling centre. People bring glass bottles and jars to the bottle bank.

The old glass is recycled and made into new glass products. These bottles are made from recycled glass.

People have recycled so many plastic bottles over the weekend that the plastic bank is now full. I make a phone call to ask someone to come and empty it.

These cups are made from recycled plastic.

Waste paper

This is a paper bank. You can post your newspapers, magazines and other paper products here.

Toilet rolls can be made from recycled paper.

It is good to meet people at the recycling bank.
This lady asks me where she can take old clothes.
I tell her where the **textile** bank is.

Lunchtime

Soon it is time for lunch. I go to a local shop to get some soup and a roll. All the food in this shop is **organic**. I like to eat healthy food.

I eat my lunch in the office with Victoria.

After lunch I do some **filing**. I have written
a report on my visit to the recycling centre.
I look for the right folder to file the report in.

School visit

This afternoon I am visiting a school to give a talk about recycling.

At schools we like to tell children about the three Rs: how to reduce, reuse and recycle waste. By following the three Rs we can reduce the amount of rubbish that is buried in **landfill sites**.

I show the children some **disposable** nappies.
These cannot be recycled.

Jessica shows the class a reusable nappy. It can be washed and used over and over again. It does not fill up landfill sites and so is much better for the environment.

Reuse and recycle

I show the children glass jars and tins that should be recycled, not thrown away.

We discuss how recycling things is better for the planet.

The children have made a poster about recycling.

Another way to reuse and recycle things is to make **compost** in the garden. I show the children a compost bin.

This special bin is cut in half to show what sort of things you can put in compost. You can compost fruit and vegetable remains, egg shells, tea bags and grass cuttings or flowers. You can't compost cooked foods like meat or bread.

More compost

Back at the office I find it is my turn to empty the office food waste bin. We collect food waste in this green bin and compost it.

I take the bin outside into the garden and empty it in our large compost bin. We also put grass cuttings, flowers and leaves in it.

20

Making compost from garden and household waste is one of the most useful things anyone can do. It is easy and costs very little in time or effort. Making compost helps reduce pollution and cuts down on landfill.

When it is ready to use you can spread it on your garden. Your plants will grow much better!

Going home

It is 5 o'clock. It is time to go home.

ENVIRONMENT AND DEVELOPMENT

I enjoy my job. I like helping people and it is good to feel I am helping to look after the environment.

Glossary

compost a mixture of rotting leaves, fruit and vegetables. Compost can be added back to the soil to make it richer.

disposable made to be thrown away after use

dispose to get rid of or throw away

environment the natural world of land, water and air around us

filing putting paperwork away in folders or files

fly-tipping leaving large amounts of rubbish in the wrong place

illegally doing something that is against the law

landfill sites places where rubbish is collected and then buried under soil

organic food that is produced without the use of fertilizers or pesticides

recycle to use something again

textile something made of fabric or cloth that has been woven or knitted

Index